Timeless tales of f___ ___ ___demption…

THE NATIVITY TRILOGY

in the A.D. Chronicles® series

by Bodie and Brock Thoene

Fourth Dawn

Herod, king of Judea, plunges deeper into madness as people
wonder, *Where is the promised liberator?* As signs appear in
the heavens, Mary of Nazareth receives an unusual visitor.

Fifth Seal

The little town of Nazareth is a long way from Jerusalem and
King Herod's evil clutches. Yet is anywhere in Judea far enough?

Sixth Covenant

Who in Bethlehem could guess that their tiny, obscure village,
populated by shepherds, would become the hinge upon which
all history turns…and the focus of a terrifying rampage?

The A.D. Chronicles® series transports readers back
in time to first century A.D.—and the most significant events
in the history of the world.

Fourth Dawn, Fifth Seal, *and* Sixth Covenant *are also available
complete and unabridged for the visually impaired at
www.familyaudiolibrary.com.*

For more information, visit www.thoenebooks.com

Discover the Truth through Fiction™

Zion Covenant series) and the miraculous rebirth of Israel and the Israeli War of Independence (The Zion Chronicles and The Zion Legacy series) are highly regarded for their historical accuracy, recognized by the American Library Association and Zionist libraries around the world, and widely used in university classrooms to teach history.

That their books have sold more than 10 million copies and won eight ECPA Gold Medallion awards affirms what millions of readers have already discovered—the Thoenes are not only master stylists but experts at capturing readers' minds and hearts.

Married for over 35 years, Bodie and Brock have four grown children and six grandchildren. Their assistance to Jews making aliyah to Israel from the countries of the former Soviet Union has been acknowledged by the nation of Israel.

The Shiloh Light Foundation (www.shilohlight-foundation.org), co-founded by the Thoenes, ships Christian literature and Bibles to prisoners and to members of the U.S. armed forces and their families. Through www.familyaudiolibrary.com, the Foundation also produces and provides low cost Christian audiobooks to those who are visually handicapped and/or learning disabled.

For more information, visit www.thoenebooks.com.

CHRISTMAS...

IS IT REALLY
WHAT YOU THINK?

One baby—
birthed in straw,
among curious sheep.
Such a humble beginning,
but this event would become
the hinge upon which
all history turns…

The Little Books of Why™

WHY A MANGER?

Bodie & Brock Thoene

PARABLE
SAN LUIS OBISPO, CALIFORNIA
OUTREACH
VISTA, CALIFORNIA

The Little Books of Why™ by Bodie and Brock Thoene are produced by Parable, 3563 Empleo Street, San Luis Obispo, CA 93401 and Outreach, Inc., 2230 Oak Ridge Way, Vista, CA 92081. Visit parable.com or outreach.com.

Printed in the United States of America
11 10 09 08 07 06
7 6 5 4 3 2 1

CONTENTS

INTRODUCTION

CHRISTMAS IN BAKERSFIELD

*Is the manger scene
a tradition, a trinket—
or something more?*

It was 1945, the first post-war Christmas in America. My mother, a grief-stricken single mom with a little daughter, boarded a train in her hometown of Akron, Ohio, and traveled to the end of the line in Bakersfield, California.

Alone and friendless in a strange city, Mama rented a tiny furnished apartment behind a garage and found a job as a waitress in the dining room of the Padre Hotel. She did not have enough money to buy a Christmas tree. But each day after work, with coins from tips, she walked a mile to the dime store and purchased one piece of a manger scene. One angel, 15 cents. Kneeling Mary, 20 cents. Joseph, 20 cents. Baby Jesus in manger, 25 cents. Wise Man on camel, 30 cents. Walking Wise Man, 25 cents. Sheep, 10 cents per head.

Mama and my sister celebrated that first Christmas far from home with the manger scene arranged on an upturned box to remind them of the joys of Christmas past. That day, she would recall later, was the loneliest day of her life.

Flash-forward fifteen years to Christmas, 1960. Mama was still in Bakersfield, but she was no longer lonely. She was happily married to Papa, had a house full of kids, and more friends than I could count. As Bing

Crosby crooned carols over the radio, we hauled boxes of ornaments and decorations down from the attic to add a festive air to the house Papa had built and where I had been born.

Though it was supposed to be a secret, bit by bit I had pieced together the poignant story of why Mama had left Akron, her first Christmas in Bakersfield, and the little dime-store manger scene. So that Christmas in 1960, I couldn't help but ask, "Why Bakersfield, Mama?"

"Because it was the farthest place on the map for which I could afford the fare," she said wistfully as we set up the manger scene on the stone mantel. "But my happy ending was waiting in Bakersfield. Your father. Your sisters and brother. You."

Sensing her sadness at reliving the memories, I changed the subject. "Why a manger?" I asked, placing a chipped plaster Wise Man on the cotton snow. Sheep and a donkey seemed to be studying Mary and Joseph and the smiling infant lying in the feed trough.

"I had to make a choice," Mama said plainly. "I couldn't afford to buy a tree, a manger scene, and a Christmas dinner."

Was that why the 1945 price tag of 10 cents was still on the base of a lamb? I wondered. "But why didn't you save up and buy a tree?"

Mama's eyes grew misty. "Because I only had so much money from tips. A nickel for serving breakfast. A dime if I was lucky. A quarter was a big tip. When I considered the cost, I knew only the manger scene would last. Every year we take down the decorations and haul the tree out to the curb for the trash man. But look, honey…Mary and Joseph. Gabriel the archangel. The Wise Men and camels. Shepherds and their lambs. All gathered to adore the baby Jesus lying in the manger. A little beat up with time, yes, but there they are. It's still the same story."

Together Mama and I sang with Bing Crosby:

"Away in a manger, no crib for a bed…
The little Lord Jesus lay down

His sweet head.
The stars in the sky look down
  where He lay,
The little Lord Jesus, asleep on the hay."

I was fascinated. This Christmas carol about a young mother traveling to a strange town sounded very familiar. Having no place to stay and no friends to help her seemed a lot like my mother's own story. Though Mama and my sister had stayed in a room behind a garage, not in a stable, the connection was strong in my mind.

"Look," Mama said, pointing at the manger scene. "It tells the true story about the birth of God's Son on earth. How Jesus came from heaven and was born in a stable, with a feed trough for His bed. The baby in the manger is what started Christmas. It *is* Christmas. That's why the manger will last on and on, long after the tree is thrown away and the toys wear out. Maybe someday you'll have children and grandchildren and you'll set up this manger scene with them."

My mind rapidly leapt with questions that would trouble me for years to come: If Jesus was the Son of God sent from heaven to save us, why was He born in such a smelly, dirty place? Why not a great palace?

If Jesus was born the King of the Jews, as the Wise Men believed and angels proclaimed, why was His birth so humble?

Why wasn't He laid in a gold crib encrusted with rubies and emeralds fit for the only Son of God, the heavenly Prince and Savior of the world?

These were questions Mama couldn't answer except to say, "Because that's just the way things are sometimes. Life was very hard in those days."

When she sighed, I knew she was thinking of her own life.

"Why a manger?" she asked. "No room in the inn, the story goes. Honey, I guess they just didn't know who Jesus was...."

WHY JESUS?

Who is this baby,
and why is His birth so important?

For to us a child is born,
to us a son is given,
and the government will be on his shoulders.
And he will be called
Wonderful Counselor, Mighty God,
Everlasting Father, Prince of Peace.
—Isaiah 9:6

Not just any baby. *Such a baby!* He'll know all the mysteries from the beginning of time. No! *Before* the beginning! All that explained! Messiah. First Light. He who sang the stars into existence will be born.

—JOSEPH IN *FIFTH SEAL*

As Joseph reflected on who the baby in the manger really was, he was in awe. Who could take everything in? Apart from the proclamations of heavenly heralds, how would anyone else accept it?

Baby Jesus, Eternal Word of the One True and Living God, pursed rosebud lips and made sucking noises. Inside the feed trough, wrapped in swaddling cloths and cocooned in a blanket, the Son of God blinked unfocused eyes at the lamp's flame.

"Shalom, little one," Joseph whispered, adoring what he saw. He rubbed the corner of his eye on his robe's sleeve.

A moment later the baby's right hand closed around Joseph's little finger. Joseph's eyes overflowed onto his cheeks and down into his beard.

"Shalom," he whispered again. "Welcome to our—" Stopping, the carpenter corrected himself. "Welcome to your world. You are loved."

—*Fifth Seal*

O, COME LET US ADORE HIM...

What is it about a Jewish boy named Jesus, born so long ago to a poor family of no influence or human importance and born among sheep, no less, that calls to our hearts, "Let's go see…" once a year?

Why do scores of shoppers crowd malls, accompanied by the strains of carols on loudspeakers proclaiming messages such as this one:

> "O come, let us adore Him!
> O come, let us adore Him!
> O, come let us adore Him!
> Christ the Lord!"

Who is the baby called by angels, "Christ the Lord," and why should we, like the shepherds of Bethlehem and the Wise Men, seek Him and adore Him?

The answer goes back to the very beginning of the world….

> In the beginning was the Word, and the Word was with God, and the Word was God. He was with God in the beginning.
>
> Through him all things were made; without him nothing was made that has been made.
>
> —JOHN 1:1-3

The Bible reveals that the Word—Jesus—existed before time and before creation. That He was not only "with God" but "was God."

Genesis 1:1 tells us, "In the beginning, God created the heavens and the earth…"

How glorious it would be to have seen the creation of the world! The fingers of God separating the heavens and the earth, the water from the land, the day from the night, and the first glittering of the stars and planets on the fresh canvas of God's world.

Jesus, the Eternal Son of God, was creator of all that. How then could the Living Word lay aside His glory and descend from heaven to earth to live as a fragile human?

It was all because of love.

Yet the Bible tells us that the wages of sin is death (Romans 6:23). How can death be our destiny if God loves us? Where did death come from?

In the Beginning, God created man and woman "in his own image" (Genesis 1:27) with a loving relationship in mind. And He saw that His original creation was "good."

Adam and Eve lived in a perfect place. The Lord walked with them and fellowshipped with them face to face. Who knows how long their lives were in perfect harmony with the Creator? They were given everything they wanted or needed and were warned by God that there was only one tree they could not eat from and if they disobeyed, they would die.

Enter Satan, the fallen angel Lucifer, who had other plans.

When Eve was tempted by the serpent, she was offered the fruit of a tree that would make her like the Almighty. She didn't need the tree for food. She could eat of all the other trees. The Lord fed Adam and Eve by His own hand. Why did she taste the fruit, knowing God had forbidden it? The temptation was that she would be "like God."

She was unwilling to let God be God in the lives of her husband and her future children. She wanted to be the one in charge. Eve believed she could act better for them than the Almighty Himself. Doubting God and needing to control our own lives and the lives of others has been the curse of mankind ever since.

> In him was life, and that life was the light of men. The light shines in darkness, but the darkness has not understood it.
>
> —JOHN 1:4-5

From that first moment of disobedience, darkness descended into the place that had once been filled with light and life and joy. Darkness descended into the hearts of the mother and father of all humankind.

THE FIRST SACRIFICE

The eyes of Adam and Eve were opened, and they realized they were naked; so they sewed fig leaves together and made coverings for themselves. But without God's help Adam couldn't repair the damage he and Eve had already done.

The Lord God called to Adam, "Where are you?"

He replied, "I heard you, so I hid. I was afraid because I was naked" (Genesis 3:7, 9-10).

The first result of sin in the heart of man was fear of God. The second result was an attempt by Adam to hide his nakedness and guilt from God. But a manmade covering of fig leaves could not hide the truth from God. On the very day that Adam disobeyed God the penalty of death had to be enforced.

Through one man, death entered the world. But there, in the Garden of Eden, God put into motion the plan that would restore to all the descendants of Adam fellowship with the Lord and Eternal Life! The Lord Himself provided the first substitutionary sacrifice for Adam's sin. The Lord killed an innocent lamb and covered the nakedness of Adam and Eve with its skin.

That lamb died in place of Adam and Eve.

"The Lord God made garments of skin for Adam and his wife and clothed them" (Genesis 3:21). Because they now knew about good and evil, God banished them from the Garden of Eden and placed "cherubim and a flaming sword flashing back and forth to guard the way to the tree of life" (Genesis 3:23-24).

Life changed drastically for Adam and Eve…and all their descendants.

Even in the midst of such darkness, all was not lost. Hope was not lost. God had a plan for redemption—for the saving of the human race. But it was a plan that would reveal itself in His timing over thousands of years. It would also cost Him the ultimate sacrifice: the life of His one and only Son, Jesus.

Jesus, whose name in Hebrew means "God is Salvation."

Jesus, the baby in the manger.

> The Word became flesh and made his dwelling among us. We have seen his glory, the glory of the One and Only, who came from the Father, full of grace and truth.
>
> —John 1:14

Almighty God could have descended as a mighty warrior, surrounded by a host of angel armies, to destroy all evil with a vengeful flash of the sword. Instead He arrived gently and quietly...in the womb of a young woman in the backwoods of Nazareth.

Mankind was not created for the sake of the world. No, the heavens and the earth were created for the sake of mankind.

The story of creation begins with the spirit of God brooding over the waters like a hen above her nest. All of creation was covered by His love. When the nest was finally perfect, man and woman were created last of all. Created to have fellowship and share in the love of God every day. He walked with them in the garden until the children He created and cherished turned from Him and followed their own way. There is no greater sorrow than the fall of man and the entry of death into a perfect world.

But here is the good news! All of Scripture points to an hour in history and to the birth of the One by whose word all of creation came into existence. If the Lord created all things because of His love for His children, does it not stand to reason that He would come personally to save everyone who calls upon His name?

For God so loved the world that he gave his
one and only Son, that whoever believes in
him shall not perish but have eternal life.
—John 3:16

All the hopes of mankind since the ban-
ishment from Eden were suddenly contained
within the womb of one young woman riding
humbly on the back of a donkey!

Some would scoff about God sending the
Messiah in the form of a baby. Others would
believe, seek Him, and worship at His feet.

But none would remain untouched. In-
deed, the whole world seemed to be waiting—
some with dread and palpable hatred, others
with hope and breathless anticipation.

Another thirty years would pass between
the birth of the Messiah and the time He finally revealed Himself to His beloved Israel.
Oppressed by the Romans and corrupt lead-
ers in Jerusalem, the people longed for the
Messiah to destroy all evil.

Then Jesus, whom the angel called Immanuel, "God-with-us," finally appeared on the scene. He was vastly different from everyone's expectations. Instead of judgment, He brought mercy and love. For over thirty years, he walked this earth...and stories of His miracles abounded.

Men who had never walked before ran after Him.

Sons who had never spoken a word sang praises to His name.

Women who had lived lonely lives, barren of hope, danced at their own weddings while others carried babies in their arms.

Beautiful daughters, once marred by leprosy, were healed and whole and reunited with families who had grieved as though their girls were dead.

It was true what the prophets had said about Messiah: Jesus healed them of all their diseases.

So it had come to pass, *"Those who have long lived in darkness have seen a great light."*

Jesus was—and is—that Light. Have you allowed Him into the dark places of your heart?

Why Jesus?

Heaven has spoken plainly about who Jesus is—from His existence before time began…to His descent to earth as a baby in the manger…to the miracles He worked while walking the earth. Every word of Holy Scripture points to Jesus as Redeemer.

But it is up to you to choose whether or not to believe.

WHY A BABY?

Thousands of years before the baby in the manger,
there was another miraculous birth…
another promised son.

When Abram was ninety-nine years old, the Lord
appeared to him and said, "I am God Almighty;
walk before me and be blameless.
I will confirm my covenant between me and you
and will greatly increase your numbers….
As for me, this is my covenant with you…
No longer will you be called Abram;
your name will be Abraham,
for I have made you
a father of many nations."

—Genesis 17:1-5

The Lord appeared to Abraham near the great trees of Mamre while he was sitting at the entrance to his tent in the heat of the day. Abraham... bowed low to the ground...

The Lord said, "I will surely return to you about this time next year, and Sarah your wife will have a son."

Now Sarah was listening at the entrance to the tent.... Abraham and Sarah were...well advanced in years. So Sarah laughed to herself as she thought, "After I am worn out and my master is old, will I now have this pleasure?"

Then the Lord said to Abraham, "Why did Sarah laugh and say, 'Will I really have a child, now that I am old?' Is anything too hard for the Lord? I will return to you at the appointed time next year and Sarah will have a son."

Sarah was afraid, so she lied and said, "I did not laugh."

But he said, "Yes, you did laugh."

—GENESIS 18:1-2, 10-15

A PROMISED SON

God's plan for saving humankind from death and restoring us to fellowship with Him is revealed throughout the Old Testament. Thousands of years before the manger, there was another miraculous birth...another promised son.

The book of Genesis tells the story of Abraham and his wife, Sarah, both of whom had grown very old without having a baby. Then, one day, God appeared to Abraham and said:

> "I will make you very fruitful; I will make nations of you, and kings will come from you. I will establish my covenant as an everlasting covenant between me and you and your descendants after you for the generations to come, to be your God and the God of your descendants after you."
>
> —Genesis 17:6-7

But this promise was made before Abraham had a son who would be his heir...and Abraham was already ninety-nine years old. Sarah was nearing ninety!

If that situation wasn't difficult enough, when God later confirmed his promise to Abraham, He even expanded its scope:

> "Abraham will surely become a great and powerful nation, and all nations on earth will be blessed through him."
>
> —GENESIS 18:18

How could that be? Abraham and Sarah had very different responses to the promise.

Although having a baby now seemed impossible, Abraham believed.

Sarah, whose Hebrew name means "Ruler," was also given the opportunity to be humbly obedient in accepting God's promise. Instead, she laughed at the impossibility of it. Like Eve, Sarah wanted to be in control. She chose not to believe that, with God, all things are possible.

Even so, God, in His mercy, fulfilled His pledge to Abraham.

> Now the Lord was gracious to Sarah as he had said, and the Lord did for Sarah what he had promised. Sarah became pregnant and bore a son to Abraham in his old age, at the very time God had promised him.
> —GENESIS 21:1-2

The promise came true! Baby Isaac—the son of promise, the son of the covenant—was born. Isaac's Hebrew name means, "He will Laugh!" Only now the family would laugh with joy, not disbelief. Miraculously and unexpectedly, everything was now going according to the plan!

Then Abraham's faith was tested in a way that would break and shape any father's heart. Here is the story, told from his son Isaac's perspective.

My father loved me very much. And I loved him. He was a very old man when I was born. I played around him like a lion cub plays with an old lion. Tugging, wrestling, sitting in his lap while he told me stories. Yes, I learned a lot sitting with him. I learned that nothing is too hard for God. He told me. Told me what God had said about my birth. That I had a future and a hope. I believed him.

One night when I was still young, I awoke to a distant rumble of thunder over the hills. I heard my father whisper, "Here I am." And I knew God was speaking to Father again. God said to my father, "Take your son, your only son, Isaac, whom you love, and go to the region of Moriah. Sacrifice him there as a burnt offering on one of the mountains I will tell you about."

At first light, Father saddled the donkey. He called me and two of his servants. Father cut the wood himself and loaded it on the donkey. He did not consult my mother. She would have tried to stop us, I believe. So off we went.

Father spoke little except to pray. He fasted and spent the long nights awake, watching over me. I woke up with him sitting beside me. Stroking my hair. "Isaac, Isaac. My son, my only son. You know how much I love you."

"Yes, Father."

On the third day, near what is now Bethlehem, Father looked up and saw Mount Moriah in the distance. He said to his servants, "Stay here with the donkey while I and the boy go over there. We will worship and then come back to you."

So Father took the wood and placed it on my shoulders to carry. He himself carried the fire and the knife. But I carried the wood alone.

After a while I noticed there was no lamb to sacrifice so I asked him, "Father?"

"Yes, my son?"

"The fire and the wood are here, but where is the lamb for the burnt offering?"

Here is a mystery revealed by the Eternal God. Father answered my question in these exact words and in this precise order as recorded in the Holy Scripture, "God He will provide Himself...God He will provide Himself...the lamb...for the burnt offering... son of me."

And so we went on together.

As we walked and the wood grew heavy on my shoulders, I thought about what my father said. The words he chose to explain sounded to me as though he meant that God would provide Himself as the sacrifice! And the lamb for the offering would be His Son! Father knew something about the future which I didn't yet understand. Is anything too hard for God? Abraham was my father, and I trusted him.

When we reached Mount Moriah, where the Temple now stands, I knew this was the place God had told him about. Father built an altar there and arranged the wood on it. He put his hands on my face and looked into my eyes. And then I knew. Suddenly I knew. I was his only son. I knew how much he loved me. How dear I was to him. His future was in me. I was the son of God's promise to him. And yet I was not afraid. Even if I died there on that altar, I trusted that nothing was too hard for God. He would raise me up again!

"My only son. I love you, my son," Father said to me.

"I love you, my father."

So I laid myself down willingly to be bound: a trusting, obedient son. My father tied me hand and foot, lest instinct make me flinch or jerk away when the knife went into my heart and the sacrifice be ruined. And he laid me on the wood.

Just as my father's hand raised above my chest, prepared to plunge in the knife, in that instant I saw! I saw a bright light! Brighter than the sun! I saw the sacrifice yet to come! I saw the face of Him who had first shown Himself to my father!

Then I heard the voice! Above us. Louder than a thunderclap. Abraham! Abraham! It was the voice of the Angel of God!

"Here I am!"

Do not lay a hand on the boy! Do not do anything to him! Now I know you fear God because you have not withheld from Me your son, your only son!

Then my eyes were opened, and I saw a ram caught by his horns in a thicket! My father went over, took the ram, and sacrificed it as an offering instead of me. So my father called that place "God Will Provide." And to this day it is said, "On the mountain of God it will be provided."

When the sun glinted on the blade of the knife and it flashed toward me, I was dead... you know? But my father received me back alive again.

Then the Angel of God called to my father from heaven a second time: *I swear by Myself, declared God, that because you have done this and not withheld your son, your only son, I will surely bless you and make your descendants as numerous as the stars in the sky and as the sand on the seashore. Your descendants will take possession of the cities of their enemies and through your offspring all nations on earth will be blessed because you have obeyed Me.*

And so this tells also of a future event. The offering of a son will be played out on the holy mountain once more. Very soon, here, in Jerusalem. This time it will be God's only Son who carries the wood on His back and provides Himself as our sacrifice. He will let Himself be bound and will lie down willingly as the Lamb to die for all of us.

This is not only the story of Abraham and Isaac, but the truth of how it will be for the Messiah, God's beloved Son, His only Son!

For God so loves the world that He gave His only Son, the Messiah, that whoever believes in Him will never die but have eternal life. On the mountain of God our salvation will be provided. He is the Lamb of God who takes away the sins of men and blesses the nations. The Messiah will carry the burden of the wood upon which He will die. He will yield to this and lay down His life willingly, knowing that He will be raised again to life after three days' journey into death. And all who call upon His name will be saved! This is the promise of Almighty God. It is all there, recorded in the Scripture, for all to read and know.

—*First Light*

Abraham's faith faced the most severe test possible…and he passed. God rewarded that faith by providing a substitute sacrifice.

But don't miss this: a sacrifice was still required! The boy Isaac was saved, but the ram caught in the thicket still had to die.

A promise made. A promise fulfilled. But never without a cost!

DO YOU BELIEVE THE PROMISE?

Thousands of years have passed since the first Temple of the Lord rose, stone by stone, on the very mountain where Abraham had offered his firstborn son as a sacrifice. Yet the story of Abraham and Isaac on Mount Moriah is as compelling today as it was when it first happened.

Are you like Sarah, laughing in disbelief at God's promises?

Do you have the faith of Abraham? He trusted completely! Believed that even if his beloved Isaac perished, God would raise his only son up to life again!

Who will walk beside the only Son of God? Who will travel up the mountain with knife held high to offer your own cherished desire and ambition on the altar of the Lord? Can you believe God's promise that He loves you enough to die in your place so you might live?

Are you like Abraham or Sarah?

WHY MARY?

The angel's words would change everything
about Mary's life.
But only she could choose how to respond.

In the sixth month, God sent the angel Gabriel
to Nazareth, a town in Galilee,
to a virgin pledged to be married to a man
named Joseph,
a descendant of David.
The virgin's name was Mary.

—LUKE 1:26-27

I'll thank Him one day for making the stars and writing His story in the heavens for everyone to see. But first, my part is a small one. I'll be His mama. Rock my baby in my arms. No cold, distant stars to hold Him. A mother's arms, warm and gentle. I'll sing Him to sleep. Sit by His cradle and be there to love Him and care for Him when all the stars have vanished and He wakes in the morning.

—MARY IN *FIFTH SEAL*

HUMBLE, OBEDIENT FAITH

For thousands of years God's plan for our salvation was waiting for the moment a young virgin in Israel would come face to face with God's messenger and demonstrate a faith like Abraham's.

Unlike Eve, Mary would say, "I am the Lord's servant." Unlike Sarah, she would proclaim, "Nothing is impossible for God!"

What must it have been like for Mary the night the angel Gabriel appeared to her?...

A blast of wind blew the barn door closed with a bang. The chimes came again, louder. A whisper: *Mary.*

"Who are you? Who's there?" Mary's heart raced. She turned her eyes to search the absolute blackness. "Is someone there?"

A sweet aroma, like that of lavender blossoms, crept in among the dusty dryness of the barn.

Mary got up and began to sing softly, as though her song could vanquish her terror: "Give thanks to the Lord, for He is good; His love endures forever."

A second voice, a deep and resonant sigh, joined in on the chorus, echoing a beat behind her song: *His love endures forever.*

"Let those who fear the Lord say"—she held up her hands—"who are you?"

A translucent glow appeared, like the view of golden dawn breaking through rain clouds. *I am Gabriel.*

She tried to sing. "His love . . ." Her words faltered and fell away.

The now identified but still mysterious voice replied in song: *His love endures forever.* With each word the gleam increased in intensity, until something—some*one*—materialized before her.

Mary dropped to her knees and cried out, "The Lord, God is with me; I will not be afraid! What can man do to me?"

A golden shape—like a man, only not a man—towered over her and the cattle. His head reached almost to the ceiling. Light and warmth emanated from his presence. Stretching out golden arms, he spoke, yet his lips did not move. *Greetings, you who are highly favored.*

She covered her head with her arms and trembled in terror. Sound and light shook her to the core.

The angel consoled her. *Do not be afraid, Mary, you have found favor with God. You will be with child and give birth to a son. And you are to give Him the name Jesus, Salvation. He will be great and will be called the Son of the Most High. God will give Him the throne of His father David. His kingdom will never end.*

"How will this be," Mary asked, "since I am a virgin?"

The Holy Spirit will overshadow you. So the holy one to be born will be called the Son of God.

Mary remembered other women of Israel who had been granted miraculous births. *Nothing is too hard for God*, she thought.

The angel seemed to hear her thoughts. *Elizabeth, your mother's sister, is going to have a child in her old age, and she who was barren is in her sixth month. For nothing...nothing...is impossible with God.*

Mary smiled at the thought of Aunt Elizabeth having a baby. Wonderful news. "I am the servant of God!" She laughed in delight. "May it be to me as you have said."

—*Fourth Dawn*

Put yourself in Mary's sandals. . . .

You have always dreamed of being married. Because you live in a day when such relationships are arranged, you accept that your father will choose your betrothed. You know of the man chosen for you; you think of him at night and wonder what your life will be like together.

Then one night you receive stunning news—from an angel, no less. His message will change everything about that future relationship...especially if your betrothed doesn't believe your account.

How would you respond? What would your heart attitude be about your present? your future?

When Mary encounters the angel in her father's barn, her attitude is, *I am yours, Lord. Anything you ask. I believe that anything is possible for you to accomplish.*

But was Mary's a blind faith? An easy faith? Certainly not! She had expected to be married shortly. To have a humble life. Certainly not a life in the spotlight. She was a woman of small dreams....

Joseph to love me. Children of my own. A small little life here in the place I grew up. That's all I have ever wanted, Lord. Who am I that You would honor me? I'm just like everyone else. And now, am I strong enough to face Papa's anger? certain disgrace? strong enough to maybe even lose Joseph, if he doesn't believe me? I am Your servant, Lord. I am. But my heart might break for it....

The morning Mary set out for Zechariah's and Elizabeth's, it was the end of life as Mary had known it. The end of pleasant childhood and drowsy dreams of a future that would have allowed her to live in the serenity of obscurity.

As Mary shouldered her pack that contained food enough for a week of travel by foot, she took one last look round to remember how it was.

The little house. Papa's workshop. The barn. The cheese room. Mary drank in the view of the familiar little farm surrounded by orchards and fields frosted with newly sprouted barley.

When will I see home again, Lord? My little sisters? Papa? Joseph? And where will You lead me between this moment and then? What adventure have You planned? I am Your servant.

Even one spring day away from Galilee seemed like too long. She would never see home again if Papa did not relent. He did not come out to say good-bye....

Mary's life plans were interrupted by an unexpected journey. Within her womb was the Messiah that Herod, king of the Jews, feared more than anyone. Yet Mary was unafraid. Each step she took toward Zechariah and Elizabeth's home was one of excitement. For at the end of the journey would be the confirmation of the angel's message.

Mary...hurried to a town in the hill country of Judea, where she entered Zechariah's home and greeted Elizabeth. When Elizabeth heard Mary's greeting, the baby leaped in her womb, and Elizabeth was filled with the Holy Spirit. In a loud voice she exclaimed: "Blessed are you among women, and blessed is the child you will bear! But why am I so favored, that the mother of my Lord should come to me? As soon as the sound of your greeting reached my ears, the baby in my womb leaped for joy."

—LUKE 1:39-44

FAVORED BY GOD

Why Mary?

When confronted with life-changing words from an angelic messenger, Mary's response was not only immediate belief, but action. She traveled to see the pregnant Elizabeth!

Mary, whose name means "bitter rebellion," would carry the promised Son of God in her womb. But, unlike Eve, Mary was no rebel. She was favored by the Lord above all women. He had searched her heart, found no bitterness there, and declared her worthy. Her humble acceptance of her role in God's eternal plan displayed a faith like Abraham's.

When the angel appeared to Mary, he brought her a word from God. Because of her belief, she received the Word into her spirit. Then, nine months later, that Eternal-Word-Made-Flesh dwelt among us. Such a miracle!

That miracle continues today. Receiving God's Word into your spirit and believing in the power of the Holy Spirit results in having God's Word present and alive in you.

As the Christmas carol "O Little Town of Bethlehem" pleads: "O holy Child of Bethlehem descend to us, we pray. Cast out our sin and enter in; be born in us today!"

WHY JOSEPH?

He was an ordinary carpenter
with a pregnant wife-to-be.
To marry her, he would have to break
all of society's rules.
But could his dreams about the baby be true?

All this took place to fulfill
what the Lord had said through the prophet:
"The virgin will be with child
and will give birth to a son,
and they will call him Immanuel"
—which means, "God with us."

—MATTHEW 1:22-23

This is how the birth of Jesus Christ came about: His mother Mary was pledged to be married to Joseph, but before they came together, she was found to be with child through the Holy Spirit. Because Joseph her husband was a righteous man and did not want to expose her to public disgrace, he had in mind to divorce her quietly.

But after he considered this, an angel of the Lord appeared to him in a dream.... When Joseph woke up, he did what the angel of the Lord had commanded him and took Mary home as his wife.

—MATTHEW 1:18-20, 24

STEP INTO JOSEPH'S SHOES...

Joseph of Nazareth, a simple carpenter, anticipated a quiet life with his soon-to-be wife, Mary, and the blessings of a flock of children. His name in Hebrew is a prayer: "Let him increase!" Joseph was honest, loved God, and helped others poorer than himself, even though his own riches were nothing to speak of. He had always sensed the approval of God in his life...until now.

How could Mary be pregnant—*before* they were married? Joseph knew *he* was not the father. So who *was* the father? Could Mary's story be true? Had an *angel* really told her that she, a virgin, would conceive "by the Holy Spirit"? Was that physically possible?

The questions made Joseph's head ache. He loved Mary. They had already gone through the customs for betrothal. But if he married her now, he'd be the laughingstock of Nazareth. Neighbors would count the months as Mary's waistline grew so soon after the wedding. There would be no doubt the timing was off. All of Nazareth would be hedging their bets on who the real father was...and would call Joseph a fool.

So what should he do? Live life alone? Or forgive Mary for her betrayal, take her in, and raise another man's child as his own? The situation was beyond Joseph's control...and beyond his understanding.

How could it be that a virgin could conceive? That this baby could be the promised Messiah? It was too much to comprehend.

Then an angel of the Lord appeared to Joseph in a dream....

There was someone—large, shadowy, undefined—standing in the corner of the room. Joseph saw him plainly, despite the lack of lamp or candle. "Who...are you?"

Shalom, Joseph, son of David.

"Why speak to me like this? I'm a poor carpenter. Son of Jacob, a poor carpenter. Of David's line, true enough, but far from palaces and kingdoms. And I am descended from the line from which a king of Israel can never be born."

Have you forgotten the prophecy your father taught you? "You have redeemed your people by your strength! The descendants of Jacob and Joseph by your might!"

"I haven't forgotten. My father taught me that our names were part of the redemption prophecies. But he couldn't have meant me? A part of that? But Mary doesn't carry a son of mine."

You have spoken correctly. But do not be afraid to take Mary as your wife, because what is conceived in her is from the Holy Spirit. She will give birth to a son, and you are to give

*Him the name Jesus, because He will save His
people from their sins.*

Joseph suddenly heard voices, roaring in a
mighty wind! He covered his face and trembled
in terror. "Who am I that a messenger would
speak to me? Who am I to imagine that I could
raise the Lord's Anointed?"

—*Fourth Dawn*

Mary and Joseph were both descendants of David but through different ancestors. Joseph's ancestor King Jeconiah was cursed for turning from the Lord, and thus Messiah could not come from his lineage. Mary's line from David remained blessed. So each played a different role in redemption. Mary would bring forth the Redeemer. Joseph was among those in David's lineage who would be redeemed.

GOD'S WONDERFUL PLAN

Joseph was from a humble lineage—a family of carpenters.

If an angel appeared to you and said, "Don't be afraid! You are a part of God's wonderful plan to save the entire world," how would you respond?

The enormity of his task pressed Joseph onto the hard cold stone. "Jesus is the Word, the Creator. And I am to be His father? I? I will carry the Son of God on *my* shoulders? Rock Him to sleep? Teach Him his alphabet, though His is the story of the Scriptures and the word that spoke worlds into existence? Teach Him to pray who is Lord of the Sabbath, existing in equal power and glory with God from the foundation of the world? Jesus, the son of a carpenter? It's too big for my mind to comprehend!"

Joseph would be protector, friend, and brother to Mary. As a carpenter, he was a man of great physical strength. His standing as a righteous man would also shield her reputation. His calm, quiet spirit would stand between her and the dark unseen force that must surely be seeking to destroy her respectability even now as she carried the Messiah in her womb.

None outside Mary's immediate family would know the true circumstances of Mary and Joseph's marriage. He wouldn't even be able to tell his closest friends about the angel's visit. They would think him crazy.

The responsibility of providing for Mary and the baby she carried was a heavy one. Joseph shouldered the burden with the prayer that he would never let The Lord of All the Angel Armies down. That meant never letting Mary down.

"Who am I, Lord, that You have chosen me?" Joseph asked.

The Lord replied, *There are stormy seas ahead. Be strong! Stand by Mary. Comfort her. You also were chosen from the dawn of creation! For this moment you were born.*

—*Fifth Seal*

Joseph—so ordinary, but gifted with humility and faith—would play a pivotal role not only for *his* generation, but all generations to come, throughout the world and for all eternity! His life is proof that God uses ordinary people to accomplish His plans. What mighty plans God may be accomplishing in *your* life at this very moment!

> "I know the plans I have for you,"
>   declares the Lord,
> "plans to prosper you and not to harm you,
> plans to give you hope and a future."
>
> —Jeremiah 29:11

All things are possible with God!

WHY BETHLEHEM?

*Why would the greatest King of all
choose this humble, out-of-the-way village—
populated by shepherds, their families,
and noisy, smelly sheep—
to be his birthplace?*

He tends his flock like a shepherd;
He gathers the lambs in his arms
And carries them close to his heart.

—Isaiah 40:11

We all, like sheep, have gone astray,
   each of us has turned to his own way;
and the Lord has laid on him
   the iniquity of us all.

He was oppressed and afflicted,
   yet he did not open his mouth;
he was led like a lamb to the slaughter,
   and as a sheep before her shearers is silent,
   so he did not open his mouth...

He poured out his life unto death,
   and was numbered with the trangressors.
For he bore the sin of many,
   and made intercession for the transgressors.

—ISAIAH 53:6-7, 12

"Bethlehem's no fit place for a king t' be born," Zadok the shepherd complained. "Only shepherds' babies born there. Common folk, every one. There's no palace there, no grand houses. Shepherds and sacrificial lambs—that's Bethlehem."

"And kings...David!" Stabbing a crooked finger down on the scroll of Micah, Simeon the scholar argued, "Yet it is clearly so: Bethlehem, birthplace of King David, who received the promise that the future King Messiah would be of his descent."

"So a child born in Bethlehem," Zadok mused. "Could it be he's already there?"

Simeon and Rabbi Eliyahu shook their heads in unison.

"Possible, but unlikely," Eliyahu intoned.

Simeon added, "Mystery upon mystery. The Son of God, whose origin is from forever past, coming to earth as a man...Son of God, but also Son of Man...a human infant. Perhaps he'll need human assistance too."

—*Fifth Seal*

"O little town of Bethlehem
how still we see thee lie.
Above thy deep and dreamless sleep
the silent stars go by.
Yet in thy dark streets shineth
the everlasting Light.
The hopes and fears of all the years
are met in thee tonight.

For Christ is born of Mary
and gathered all above.
While mortals sleep, the angels keep
their watch of wondering love.
O morning stars together
proclaim the holy birth.
And praises sing to God the King
and Peace to men on earth.

O holy Child of Bethlehem
descend to us, we pray.
Cast out our sin and enter in
be born in us today.
We hear the Christmas angels
the great glad tidings tell.
O come to us, abide with us
our Lord Emmanuel."
—PHILLIPS BROOKS, 1868

O LITTLE TOWN
OF BETHLEHEM

Ask anyone who celebrates Christmas where the Christ-child was born, and most will name Bethlehem. Carols like "O Little Town of Bethlehem" memorialize its fame. Many could also explain why dusty, insignificant Bethlehem was chosen for such an important event. In Hebrew, Bethlehem means "House of Bread." It was prophesied that Messiah, "the Bread sent down from heaven to feed the souls of mankind," would be a descendent of King David. He would also be born in the same city where David, the shepherd-king of Israel, was born—Bethlehem!

> You, Bethlehem Ephrathah,
>   though you are small among the clans of Judah,
> out of you will come for me
>   one who will be ruler over Israel,
> whose origins are from of old,
>   from ancient times.
>   —MICAH 5:2

The bawling of sheep rang across the fields of Bethlehem. Migdal Eder, the Tower of the Flock, was the place where lambs destined for the Temple were born and raised. Every firstborn male lamb from the area around Bethlehem was considered holy, set aside for sacrifice in Jerusalem. Generations of hereditary shepherds tended the sacred flocks. They were common folk, used to many cold, lonely nights in the fields. As protectors of the sheep, they risked their lives to keep the animals from going astray...and falling into the many ravines of the hill country.

After pouring their lives out into their flocks, the shepherds would separate the lambs, choosing only the perfect firstborn males to drive to Jerusalem. There the lambs would be purchased by those who wished to atone for their sins. On the same mountain where Abraham had offered his son to the Lord, the lambs would shed their blood and lose their lives as that atonement.

It was an endless cycle.

When Christ came into the world, he said:

"Sacrifice and offering you did not desire,
   but a body you prepared for me,
with burnt offerings and sin offerings
   you were not pleased.
Then I said, 'Here I am—it is written about
   me in the scroll— I have come to do your
   will, O God.'"

—HEBREWS 10:5-7

John the Baptist called Jesus not only the "Son of God" (John 1:34) but also the "Lamb of God" (John 1:36).

The Firstborn Lamb of God would sacrifice his life to atone for the sins of all—a one-time perfect sacrifice, offered by the Father God Himself.

Where else would "the Lamb of God, who takes away the sin of the world" (John 1:29) have to be born if not Bethlehem, among the sacred Temple flocks?

But the way in which the Lamb would arrive remained a mystery to be solved.

He is coming for your sake, the angel Gabriel told Joseph. *You are chosen because you are like all those who live under the curse of exile from the presence of God. You are like every lost lamb who longs to be found by God and forgiven and carried home in the arms of the Good Shepherd.*

Joseph sighed. "Oh, that he would carry me!"

First you will carry Him.

The smell of the unfamiliar incense intensified. Wood and blossom intermingled. Commonplace and holy entwined, inseparable.

Just as the coming of the Son of God to earth as the Son of Man would be. Commonplace and holy entwined, inseparable.

It was a mystery too great to unravel, Joseph thought. "Me? How am I to carry one so great?"

In your arms. On your shoulders. Sometimes on your back. He will be very small for a while. And as fragile as a newborn lamb.

—FOURTH DAWN

"Don't make the same mistake as others," Simeon warned. "They read of what Messiah will do as king—defeating Israel's enemies and purifying the worship of the Lord—and fail to understand that he comes first as a child." Simeon clapped one aged hand on Zadok's shoulder and the other on Eliyahu's. "And you shepherds may be the first to greet him!"

—FIFTH SEAL

There had been so many years of longing for the Messiah to come and avenge the wrongs of a depraved world.

So many years of hoping for the fall of evil rulers…and the revealing of the One who would be King forever.

So many years of waiting in expectant hope…and never seeing an answer.

Yet when Messiah did come, who in all Israel knew it? Only a handful were aware of the miracle, and most of them were common folk—the humble shepherds of Bethlehem.

Why would Messiah choose to arrive in such an out-of-way place as Bethlehem? And why would the shepherds be the first to greet him?

Even this was in God's eternal plan.

> "I will place shepherds over them who will tend them, and they will no longer be afraid or terrified, nor will any be missing," declares the Lord.

> "The days are coming...
>   when I will raise up to David a righteous Branch,
> a King who will reign wisely
>   and do what is just and right in the land."
> —JEREMIAH 23:4-5

The greatest King of all would arrive in Little Bethlehem, the City of David, the city of shepherds. The place where sacrificial lambs were born and raised. He was placed in a manger. What did that sign mean to the shepherds? What does it mean to you today?

WHY A MANGER?

The fragile Lamb of God
lying in the straw
would pay the ultimate cost for our redemption.

"I am coming, and I will live among you,"
declares the Lord.
—ZECHARIAH 2:10

It was all so ordinary seeming. This was not a palace or a fortress; it was a cave. The air was warm and moist with the breath of sheep and lambs and smelled of wool and manure, not incense and costly perfume. The teenage mother was not dressed like royalty. Her protector was clearly one of the people of the land.

And yet . . .

There was the baby, wrapped in cloths and lying in a manger, even as the angel had foretold.

The accuracy of that fulfillment could not be doubted, which meant...

Head bowed, tears streamed down the shepherd's furrowed cheeks. "My Savior and my Lord."

—*Fifth Seal*

Have you declared, "My Savior and my Lord"?

CHRISTMAS IN THE LAMBING BARN

It was Christmas 1985.

I was grown and had a family of my own. We stood together inside the lambing barn as the vet shook his head sadly over the orphan lamb who bleated miserably beside its mother. She had been a beautiful young ewe our son Jake had hoped to show in 4-H. Now she was dead. How would her baby survive?

We looked hopefully into the pen across the corridor.

It had been a hard night for our flock. Our oldest ewe had also given birth. Her lamb was stillborn. She fussed and worried over her limp baby, trying to rouse him.

Maybe she would adopt the orphan.

We attempted in vain to present the motherless lamb to the grieving ewe, but she would not accept the baby. She growled and stamped her hooves and ran the little fellow into the corner. Brock snatched him up a moment before she trampled him.

"Why, Mama?" nine-year-old Jake asked me. "A dead lamb in the old girl's pen. Why won't she take the poor little guy?"

I wrapped my arms around Jake. "He isn't her own, and she knows it." I looked at the forlorn creature in my husband's arms, then at the stillborn baby.

The vet attempted to calm the angry ewe. He rubbed his head and said, "There's one thing left, if you're up for it. The shepherds used to know a trick to help an orphan lamb be adopted by a different mother. But it isn't pretty. It means hiding the live lamb beneath the fleece of the dead lamb."

We all agreed it was worth a try. While Jake and I comforted the grieving mother sheep, Brock and the vet removed both lambs. When they returned, the orphan was swaddled in the fleece of the ewe's offspring. Once again we offered the orphan lamb to the ewe. Just as the shepherds from ancient times would have done, we placed the lamb in the feed trough for the adoptive mother to discover on her own.

The mother sniffed, catching the scent of her baby's fleece. Then, with a joyful bawl, she began to lick the orphan as if he were her own! She nudged him hard, pushing him out of the manger and directing him toward his first supper. He began to nurse immediately!

We all knew everything would be all right.

"Merry Christmas!" Brock hugged Jake and me. "Once again we find life in the manger."

Covered by the fleece of another, the baby was welcomed, loved, and accepted by the ewe. She didn't seem to notice he was not her own. Or if she did, it no longer mattered to her. She adopted him without question.

It was, I thought, as I observed the happy scene, a special gift God had given us that harsh winter's night. For it was a perfect symbol of how Jesus, the Lamb of God, by His own death covers our sin and makes us acceptable to our heavenly Father.

At that moment I remembered something my mother had said about the manger scene. "It tells the true story about the birth of God's Son on earth…Jesus…was born in a stable, with a feed trough for His bed. The baby in the manger is what started Christmas. It *is* Christmas. That's why the manger will last on and on…."

You are all sons of God through faith in Christ
Jesus, for all of you who were baptized into
Christ have clothed yourself with Christ.
—GALATIANS 3:26-27

Instead of revealing His plan to priests
and rulers, God chose to show Himself first
in human form among simple shepherds who
would have understood from experience
among the flocks the sacrificial meaning of a
newborn lamb lying in a manger. *One must die
that another would live.*

Instead of arriving with great fanfare,
Messiah arrived quietly, as a firstborn
male lamb among the sacrificial flocks of
Migdal Eder.

Instead of surrounding Himself with the
glory and majesty of Jerusalem, a city that
boasted many wonders of the world, Messiah arrived among the aromas of sheep in
humble Bethlehem. The same village where
the boy David had tended sheep before he became the king of all Israel.

GOOD NEWS OF GREAT JOY!

There were shepherds living out in the fields nearby, keeping watch over their flocks at night. An angel of the Lord appeared to them, and the glory of the Lord shone around them, and they were terrified. But the angel said to them, "Do not be afraid. I bring you good news of great joy that will be for all the people. Today in the town of David a Savior has been born to you; he is Christ the Lord. This will be a sign to you: You will find a baby wrapped in cloths and lying in a manger."

Suddenly a great company of the heavenly host appeared with the angel, praising God and saying,

"Glory to God in the highest,
    and on earth peace to men on whom
    his favor rests."

When the angels had left them and gone into heaven, the shepherds said to one another, "Let's go to Bethlehem and see this thing that has happened, which the Lord has told us about."

So they hurried off and found Mary and Joseph, and the baby, who was lying in the manger. When they had seen him, they spread the word concerning what had been told them about this child, and all who heard it were amazed at what the shepherds said to them. The shepherds returned, glorifying and praising God for all the things they had heard and seen, which were just as they had been told.

—Luke 2:8-20

THE ULTIMATE SACRIFICE

Because of Eve's failure, humankind was separated from God. Eve's husband followed after her, rejecting God's one command. As a result, death entered the world as the first lamb was sacrificed in order to make clothing for Adam and Eve.

In spite of her unbelief, Sarah birthed a miracle baby...the same miracle baby that God later asked Abraham to sacrifice on Mount Moriah. Abraham, heart aching with the thought of losing his son, obeyed. At the last minute, God halted the progress of the knife in Abraham's hand, saying that He Himself would provide the sacrifice (Genesis 22:1-19).

Generations upon generations later, an angel called on Mary, the young virgin foretold in the Old Testament prophecies. He gave her the Lord's good news and asked if she was willing to believe His promises. Could Mary, like Abraham, believe that even if her beloved son died on a cross He would be raised from death? Would she walk the Way of Sorrow with Him?

God provided more than the ram caught in the thicket on Mount Moriah. God sent Jesus, His one and only Son, to earth in the form of a fragile baby to lie in a manger. And the time in history that He chose to do so couldn't have been more dangerous.

King Herod's madness and evil had begun to spread. Thus far the brutal purge in Jerusalem had resulted in the arrest and trial of Herod's sons and the murder of over two hundred others. For how long would the little village of Bethlehem remain untouched?

Knowing well about Herod's murderous rampages, Zechariah and Elizabeth had to flee from the mad king's territory with their miracle baby, John. Mary and Joseph, although loved and accepted among the people of Bethlehem, realized their great responsibility to keep baby Jesus safe. After Joseph was warned by an angel of Herod's plot to kill baby Jesus, the young family fled to safer shores.

The shepherds who saw the angels the night of Jesus' birth, heard the message of divine deliverance, and welcomed the baby, born in the City of David, into their own flock in Bethlehem, paid the ultimate cost. The shepherds' sons were slaughtered by Herod's soldiers in his rampage against all boys two and under. And the sounds of horror and mourning spread across all of little Bethlehem.

These deaths foreshadowed the sacrifice to come. Thirty-three years later God, too, paid the ultimate price—His only Son. The Firstborn Lamb of God, innocent and perfect, would die as a sacrificial Lamb to take away the sins of the world...yours and my sins.

FOUND AND FORGIVEN?

Salvation is not cheap. Its cost is beyond human measure. But it is free to all who ask.

Jesus—the God-baby who left heaven to be born in a manger, who later was crucified on a cross for you—holds up His nail-scarred hands and beckons you. How will you respond?

Like Eve, deciding to go your own way?

Like Sarah, laughing in disbelief?

Like Abraham, offering God your most cherished dreams and trusting Him?

Like Joseph, accepting that God has a plan for your life?

Like Mary, receiving God's gift of Life with open arms and a believing heart?

Like the shepherds of Bethlehem, rejoicing and embracing the newborn Lamb of God as the sacrifice for your sins?

What, really, is Christmas to you? Is it simply a time of year when you unpack the manger scene, hear Christmas carols in the malls, and enjoy the vivid reds and greens for a few weeks, then pack away all the clutter until next year? Or does the reality of Christmas remain in your heart and life all year long?

Everything in life turns on the moment Jesus, the Son of God, was born. Why not seek to know Him better?

> "If you seek Him, He will be found by you."
> —1 CHRONICLES 28:9

Jesus is not only the Lamb of God who covers our guilt with His innocence, He is the loving shepherd who longs to carry you home to safety! Have you ever felt like an orphan lamb? Like a lame lamb? Are you longing for safe pasture? To be found by God and forgiven? To be carried in His arms?

Why not call out to Jesus, the Good Shepherd, today?

IT'S ALL ABOUT YOU!

It's not enough to understand *why* the Son of God was born in a manger. It's not enough to know *Who* the baby sleeping in the stable was. It's not even enough to understand that He came as the perfect Lamb of God, the final sacrifice for your sins.

The manger is all about God's love for you, personally, as his dear child. Jesus set aside the glory of heaven to be born on earth for *you!* Jesus lived the perfect, sinless life we were meant to live before we turned away from God. He died on the cross for your sins so you can once again have a relationship with our perfect creator.

Then He rose from death. After lying in a tomb for three days, He got up and walked out of the darkness as proof that He has conquered death forever!

Now God wants you to know Him and call Him Father.

Right now He is calling your name and asking, "Where are you?"

Are you, like Adam, hiding from God because you want to hang on to your sin? "I knew it was You, God, but I was afraid so I hid!"

Through the baby in the manger, the Lamb of God will take away your sin once and for all. Listen! The heavenly Father calls to your heart: *Do not be afraid! I have come to you today with good news. My son, Jesus Christ, was born to set you free from the burden of your sin. I love you so much I gave my only Son to die in your place so that you can have Eternal Life! Don't be afraid!*

Why a manger? This, then, is the answer:

For God so loved the world (you) that he gave his only Son (Jesus), so that whoever believes in him will not perish, but have eternal life!

—JOHN 3:16

RECEIVING GOD'S GIFT

Why not answer God's call? Receive His free gift of Eternal Life! Simply pray:

> "I am no longer afraid of you, Lord. I will not hide from you. Here I am, Lord, take all my life. Forgive my sin. Teach me to do your will. Fill my heart with yourself. Be born in me today. Change me forever. Use my life for your purpose. I accept Jesus as my Savior and Shepherd. Right now I embrace the baby in the manger as my Redeemer and Lord!"

If you just prayed these words, you are now a Christian. This is His promise to you:

> If we confess our sins, he is faithful and just and will forgive us our sins and purify us from all unrighteousness.
>
> —1 John 1:9

God says you are forgiven! You are set free! You have Eternal Life!

THE MOMENT OF A LIFETIME

Why not record this moment when your life
changed for all eternity?

My Response

I believe Jesus Christ came from heaven
to die as a sacrifice for my sins.
Today I asked Him to come into my heart
and to change my life.

_____

my signature

_____

date

WHAT NEXT?

You have trusted your life to the loving hands of the Good Shepherd. Your sins are forgiven. Your heart is as clean as a newborn baby's! You are born again and the Lord promises you have Eternal Life!

You ask, "What do I do now?"

Here are three easy steps to help you as you begin your new life in Christ.

#1 Tell someone.

Since you are now a child of God, call or e-mail a Christian friend *right now!* Tell him or her that you have asked Jesus to come into your heart! Or e-mail us: brockandbodie@ littlebooksofwhy.com. We'll celebrate with you and pray for you.

> Let us hold unswervingly to the hope we profess, for he who promised is faithful.
>
> —Hebrews 10:23

#2 Begin reading the Bible.
Read the true story of Jesus, who died in your place. There is one book you can trust above all others to give you the *truth* about Jesus—the Bible. If any book disagrees with these God-breathed words, it is *not* the truth.

Begin by reading the Gospel of John. There are many modern translations that make the story even more understandable.

> All Scripture is God-breathed and is useful for teaching, rebuking, correcting and training in righteousness, so that the man of God may be thoroughly equipped for every good work.
> —2 TIMOTHY 3:16

#3 Find fellowship.
You are a child in the family of God, but you need to join in family gatherings. Alone, you cannot grow. Find a Bible-believing church where you can experience joy and fellowship and learn exactly what God's Word wants you to know about life.

> Let us not give up meeting together...but let
> us encourage one another.
>
> —HEBREWS 10:25

Tell the pastor you want to be baptized
(Galatians 3:25-27).

From these small steps the Good Shepherd
will lead you to safe pastures. Almighty God
loved you so much He was born in a stable,
lived, died, and rose from death for your sake.

There is so much of life to be lived beyond the manger. We pray your heart will
be filled with the peace and joy of that first
Christmas.

Just as there is no doubt that Christ the
Savior, the Lamb of God, was born and laid
in the manger in Bethlehem, you may be
certain that Jesus is born in your heart *today!*

> Yet to all who received him, to those who
> believed in his name, he gave the right to be-
> come children of God—children born not of
> natural descent, nor of human decision...but
> born of God.
>
> —JOHN 1:12-13

ABOUT THE AUTHORS

For over twenty-five years Bodie and Brock Thoene (pronounced Tay-nee) have pursued advanced studies in Jewish history, concentrating on the Jewish roots of Christianity. They have served as adjunct professors with The Masters College in European history, English literature, and Journalism. They also teach Writing for Publication in association with the University of the Nations, Kona, Hawaii.

Brock holds advanced degrees in History and Education. Besides being an amateur astronomer, he has made the study of biblical Hebrew his life's work. Bodie has degrees in Journalism and Communications. She began her writing career with John Wayne's Batjac Productions.

The Thoenes have written over 45 works of internationally acclaimed historical fiction—including The Zion Chronicles, The Zion Covenant, The Zion Legacy, The Shiloh Legacy, The Galway Chronicles, A.D. Chronicles, and Legends of the West—as well as regular devotional blogs and commentaries. Their weblog can be found at www.thoenebooks.com.

Their novels of pre-World War II Europe (The